A STORY TO TACO BOUT

THE DISH ON THE DISH: A HISTORY OF YOUR FAVORITE FOODS

JULIE KNUTSON

CHERRY LAKE PRESS

Published in the United States of America by Cherry Lake Publishing Group
Ann Arbor, Michigan
www.cherrylakepublishing.com

Reading Adviser: Beth Walker Gambro, MS, Ed., Reading Consultant, Yorkville, IL
Photo Credits: © fstop123/iStock.com, cover, 1; © Joshua Resnick/Shutterstock.com, 5; © fcafotodigital/
    iStock.com, 6; © Nickolas warner/Shutterstock.com, 7; © patoouu pato/Shutterstock.com, 9;
    © PamelaJoeMcFarlane/iStock.com, 10; © Marcos Castillo/Shutterstock.com, 13; © Larisa Blinova/
    Shutterstock.com, 14; © Foxys Forest Manufacture/Shutterstock.com, 17; © gowithstock/
    Shutterstock.com, 18; © Louno Morose/Shutterstock.com, 21; © David Tonelson/Shutterstock.com, 23;
    © Brannon_Naito/Shutterstock.com, 24; © Stepanek Photography/Shutterstock.com, 27; © knape/
    iStock.com, 28

Library of Congress Cataloging-in-Publication Data
Names: Knutson, Julie, author.
Title: A story to taco bout / Julie Knutson.
Description: Ann Arbor, Michigan : Cherry Lake Publishing, [2022] | Series: The dish on the dish: a history
    of your favorite foods | Includes index. | Audience: Grades 4-6
Identifiers: LCCN 2021006179 (print) | LCCN 2021006180 (ebook) | ISBN 9781534187283 (hardcover) |
    ISBN 9781534188686 (paperback) | ISBN 9781534190085 (pdf) | ISBN 9781534191488 (ebook)
Subjects: LCSH: Tacos. | Mexican American cooking. | LCGFT: Cookbooks.
Classification: LCC TX836 .K59 2022 (print) | LCC TX836 (ebook) | DDC 641.84—dc23
LC record available at https://lccn.loc.gov/2021006179
LC ebook record available at https://lccn.loc.gov/2021006180

Cherry Lake Publishing Group would like to acknowledge the work of the Partnership for 21st Century
Learning, a Network of Battelle for Kids. Please visit http://www.battelleforkids.org/networks/p21
for more information.

Printed in the United States of America
Corporate Graphics

ABOUT THE AUTHOR

Julie Knutson is an author who lives in northern Illinois with her husband, son, and border
collie. She prefers her pancakes with Nutella and bananas, her pizza "Detroit-style," and her
mac 'n' cheese with little green peas.

TABLE OF CONTENTS

First Plating

They're a **staple** of Tuesday dinners across the world. Their yummy ingredients include lettuce, shells, cheese, beans, and meat. The possibilities are endless!

You guessed it . . . we're talking about TACOS!

What's the history of this beloved handheld food? Where did tacos come from? How long have people been eating them? When and how did they become popular enough to inspire children's books and songs?

Norway celebrates eating tacos on Fridays instead of Tuesdays.

Some people prefer the crunch of a hard shell.

Corn tortillas are baked on a stovetop.

Let's start with the foldable shell that holds it all together—the **tortilla**. Thousands of years ago, ancient people of **Mesoamerica** experimented with the native plant **maize**, or corn. They cultivated it to make it more edible, more nutritious, and more **prolific**. Maize became the crop on which their civilization was built. It was commonly formed into round tortillas. These flatbreads could be folded and filled with fruits, vegetables, and meats.

If you define a taco as a flat, handheld tortilla filled with ingredients and folded, then people have been eating tacos for a very, very long time. But when and how did the name "taco" get assigned to this food? There are a few theories. One idea is that it comes from the **Nahuatl** word *tlahco*, meaning "half" or "in the middle." Another theory says that the word came out of Mexico's silver industry. In the 18th century, taco referred to explosives used to **excavate** mines. These non-edible tacos were made of paper wrapped around gunpowder. Miners stuck the cylinders

*How important was maize to ancient Mesoamericans? Mythology gives us some clues. According to a Maya creation myth, the first humans were formed out of **masa** dough. Today in Mexico and Central America, masa tortillas are an essential, life-sustaining food.*

Jalapeño peppers are used to add spice to different dishes.

Tacos are popular street food.

into holes in mine walls and lit them. The resulting explosion shook loose the silver ore. Miners often brought tortillas to work to fill and eat. It's believed they named the food "taco" because of the resemblance between the two items.

As Mexico became industrialized in the 19th century, migrants moved from rural areas to cities in search of jobs. The largest, Mexico City, drew people from around the country. Workers needed portable lunches that could be bought on the street and eaten without silverware. *Taquerías*, often operated by women migrants who brought their regional cooking styles to the city, sprung up in factory neighborhoods. Within one city, people could now try foods from all around the country. In the years to come, these food traditions spread even further north. They reached cities like Los Angeles, California, and San Antonio, Texas.

Corn Chemistry, 101

Corn is a staple crop in the Americas. But a corn-based diet doesn't provide enough vitamins. People eating mainly corn may get a life-threatening disease called **pellagra**. To provide needed nutrients and make corn more digestible, ancient peoples developed a process called **nixtamalization**.

First, corn kernels are soaked in a bath of water mixed with a substance like limestone or wood ash. That releases calcium and niacin, also called vitamin B3, in the kernels. Next, the kernels are cooked. They're then steeped in the liquid, rinsed, and finally ground down into cornmeal, or *masa harina*.

Masa flour can be patted into dough and cooked up to make deliciously flat, round tortillas . . . the perfect building block for your other taco ingredients!

CHAPTER 2

Migrations

Large portions of the United States were part of Mexico until 1848. This area included lands in Arizona, California, Colorado, Nevada, New Mexico, Texas, and Utah. After the Mexican-American War, national borders moved. This change paved the way for meetings between people who'd lived in the Southwest for generations and **Anglo** settlers. In the late 19th and early 20th centuries, immigrants also came from Mexico to cities like Los Angeles, California.

Tacos al pastor are tacos made with **spit**-grilled meat.

There are many different options for salsas to top your tacos, including mild tomato and corn salsa.

Similar to Italian immigrants who came to the United States around the same time, Mexican-Americans adapted recipes to the ingredients they could find. Cheddar cheese, wheat flour, ground beef, and shredded lettuce all made their way into the taco. As with other cuisines, Mexican food was enjoyed in immigrant neighborhoods and in regions with large Mexican populations.

Chili Queens of San Antonio

Tacos weren't the first Mexican food to gain a following with Anglo populations in the United States. In the late 1800s and early 1900s, *chili con carne* and tamales both became popular. On weekend nights, the rich smells of chili, beans, and tamales would waft across Texas plazas. The aromas came from the pots of the city's "Chili Queens," who set up booths at busy marketplaces. These **entrepreneurs** often supported their families with the money they made from their food stands.

But the idea of eating, drinking, and socializing in a public square wasn't popular with everyone. By the late 1930s and early 1940s, politicians and health officials cracked down on street food sales. This sent the Chili Queens—and the culture surrounding them—indoors.

After World War II, the United States enjoyed a period of increased wealth. During this post-war boom, people had more free time. Americans developed a taste for new foods and drinks, ranging from pizza to tiki beverages. They also became more interested in restaurant meals. Fast food was on the rise. In this environment, businessman Glen Bell saw an opportunity.

In 1950, Bell opened Bell's Burgers & Hot Dogs in a Mexican neighborhood in San Bernardino, California. It was across the street from a well-established restaurant that served tacos, the Mitla Cafe. Bell saw long lines and happy customers at Mitla. He befriended the owners and worked his way into the kitchen. He learned the restaurant's recipes and took them to launch a new business. That new business eventually became Taco Bell®.

After World War I, the centuries-old Ottoman Empire collapsed. As a result, many people from former Ottoman lands immigrated elsewhere. People who came to Mexico from Lebanon brought their food traditions, like cooking meat on a rotating spit. In the city of Puebla, this way of preparing meat made its way into the taco. Today's taco al pastor *is the result of this fusion.*

Tacos can be filled with many different proteins from grilled chicken to shrimp.

Mexico is the country that consumes the most tacos in the world.

Taco Bell®'s strategy was to bring fast-food tacos to Anglo audiences. By the mid-1960s, that approach was working. The July 3, 1966, edition of Phoenix's *Arizona Republic* reported Taco Bell® was quickly expanding its **franchise** locations. By year's end, the article noted, there would be 31 restaurants in Arizona. Another 50 were expected in Texas and New Mexico. Why did the chain grow so quickly? As Robert Campbell, head of Taco Bell®'s Arizona operations, told the reporter, "People are in a hurry . . . and they can slip in and get a bit to eat and leave."

Today, there are more than 7,000 Taco Bell® locations worldwide. They're located in cities ranging from London, England, to Mumbai, India.

Taco Bell® is known for its hard shell tacos. These differ from traditional tacos served in soft tortillas. While many think that Glen Bell invented the shelf-stable hard shell, that's not the case. Patents for fried, U-shaped tacos were filed in multiple locations in the late 1940s, well before Bell got into the taco business.

CHAPTER 3

Evolution and Wild Variations

At all times of the day, almost anywhere in the world, you can enjoy a taco. Let's take a tour to see what gets folded in tortillas in different parts of the world!

Rise and shine in Austin, Texas, birthplace of the breakfast taco. Most breakfast tacos wrap up morning mainstays like eggs and bacon in a tortilla. You can add cheese and potatoes or choose something a little more experimental. Smoked brisket or spicy **migas**, anyone?

Tostadas are similar to tacos, but their shells are flat.

Head west to Los Angeles, California. Start on Olvera Street, where you can sample tacos from a number of restaurants. Cielito Lindo has been making their specialty **taquitos**—beef wrapped in a fried corn tortilla—for more than 80 years. While in California, make a separate trip to San Bernardino. Visit Mitla Cafe, the famous restaurant still standing across the street from Glen Bell's original hamburger stand.

Down the California coast, we reach Baja, Mexico. Along the Pacific, you can expect some delicious fish tacos. Fish tacos generally come in a corn tortilla. They often are garnished with cabbage slaw, a touch of lime, and salsa.

Back in 2007, a character on Nickelodeon's iCarly *faced a dinner choice: tacos or spaghetti? He couldn't make up his mind, so he made a spaghetti taco! To the surprise of the show's creators, this wild mash-up actually gained a real-world following. What do you think? Would you try it?*

Rice and beans are popular sides that come with tacos.

In Mexico City, you can enjoy tacos in places ranging from street vendors to fancy restaurants. Choose from endless types, including slow-cooked *barbacoa*, grilled *carne asada*, or spit-fired *al pastor*. If you don't eat meat, you can opt for vegetarian or vegan options, made with soy *carnitas*!

If it's a Friday, hop on a flight to Scandinavia. It's hard to believe, but Taco Friday, or Taco Freitag, is a popular occasion in both Sweden and Norway. It's estimated that 44 percent of Norwegians eat tacos at least once a week!

In California, birria tacos are popular. Birria is a Mexican stew.

Head south to Europe's boot, Italy. Try a piada—a flatbread wrapped around ingredients like meat, cheese, and tomatoes—and ask yourself, "Just what is a taco?"

Next, it's off to Seoul, South Korea. Korean-Mexican fusion food started in Los Angeles but can now also be found in Asia. Korean-style barbecue meats and **kimchi** garnish on your tacos, anyone?

Close out the global exploration of tacos in Melbourne, Australia. In recent years, Mexican food has taken off in the land down under. Some restaurants are even making their own corn tortillas and filling them with traditional and new ingredients alike!

CHAPTER 4

Make Your Own!

Tacos are a blank canvas. Have you ever had a dessert taco? Use your imagination to transform a tortilla into your own unique creation!

INGREDIENTS:

- 6 flour tortillas
- 1 teaspoon (4 grams) cinnamon
- 1 teaspoon (4 g) sugar
- Softened butter
- 2 sliced bananas
- 12 sliced strawberries
- ⅔ cup (85 g) blueberries
- Vanilla ice cream
- Whipped cream
- Chocolate syrup

Dessert tacos can be topped with chocolate and nuts.

DIRECTIONS:

1. Gather and prepare your ingredients. Have an adult help you with slicing the fruit.

2. Brush your tortillas with butter. Sprinkle cinnamon and sugar on top. Microwave for 30 seconds.

3. Scoop ice cream into your warm tortillas. Add fruit.

4. Top with chocolate syrup and whipped cream. Enjoy!

Tacos are a great dish to share with family and friends.

10 SpecTACOular Facts

- The largest taco ever made was assembled in 2003 in Mexicali, Mexico. The massive, meat-filled creation weighed 1,654 pounds (750 kilograms)!

- The magazine *Texas Monthly* has a designated taco editor.

- The first photo ever uploaded to Instagram was taken at a taco stand in Baja, Mexico. The photo was of a golden retriever puppy.

- In the United States, National Taco Day is celebrated every October 4.

- Americans eat an estimated 4.5 billion tacos per year.

- There are more than 7,000 Taco Bell® locations in the world.

- The longest line of tacos ever—2,017 in a row—was formed at a college campus in Chadron, Nebraska, in April 2017.

- A 2012 study in Norway showed that 400,000 of Norwegians eat tacos every Friday.

- The oldest continually operating Mexican restaurant in the United States is El Charro in Tucson, Arizona. They've been serving up their original recipe—ground beef tacos garnished with peas, radishes, and cheese—since 1922.

- Taco Bell® wasn't the only fast-food chain to come out of San Bernardino, California. The McDonald brothers opened their hamburger stand in the same town in 1940.

Timeline

1500 BCE Archaeological evidence suggests that nixtamalization was used to enhance the digestibility and nutritional value of corn.

Late 19th century Industrialization draws people from all over Mexico to Mexico City. Regional taco varieties travel with migrants to the city.

1891 "Taco" makes its printed debut in a novel by Manuel Payno.

1893 After thousands of Anglo visitors come to the World's Fair in Chicago, Illinois, a tamale trend takes the United States by storm.

1920s In Puebla, Mexico, Mexican and Middle Eastern food traditions combine in *tacos árabes*, later called *tacos al pastor*.

1940s Multiple Mexican-American restaurant owners, including Joseph Pompa of Arizona and Juvencio Maldonado of New York, apply for patents to develop hard shell tacos.

1950 Bell's Burgers & Hot Dogs opens in San Bernardino, California. The food stand eventually becomes Taco Bell®.

1968 Congressman Henry B. Gonzalez of San Antonio, Texas, proposes that October 4 be named National Taco Day in the United States.

1974 In Los Angeles, California, Raul Martinez converts an ice cream truck into a taco truck. The truck was so popular that he opened a restaurant, King Taco, within 6 months. Today, King Taco is a multi-million dollar chain with 22 locations.

2010 The United Nations Educational, Scientific, and Cultural Organization (UNESCO) designates Mexico's food heritage as a cultural treasure.

Further Reading

BOOKS

Hankin, Rosemary. *A Mexican Cookbook for Kids.* New York, NY: PowerKids Press, 2014.

McDaniel, Jan. *Zesty and Colorful Cuisine: The Food of Mexico.* Broomall, PA: Mason Crest, 2015

Ward, Karen. *Fun with Mexican Cooking.* New York, NY: PowerKids Press, 2010.

WEBSITES

ASKSmithsonian—Where Did the Taco Come From?
www.smithsonianmag.com/arts-culture/where-did-the-taco-come-from-81228162
Read this article to learn more about the origin of the taco.

Wonderopolis—What Is Masa?
www.wonderopolis.org/wonder/what-is-masa
Check out this website and learn all about masa.

Wonderopolis—Where Was Chili Invented?
www.wonderopolis.org/wonder/where-was-chili-invented
Check out this website and learn about the history of chili.

GLOSSARY

Anglo (AN-gloh) a term used to describe white settlers of European ancestry in the southwest United States

entrepreneurs (on-truh-pruh-NURZ) people who start businesses or create products

excavate (ek-SKUH-vayt) to dig out and remove

franchise (FRAN-chize) a company's license to an individual to own and operate one of their businesses

kimchi (KIM-chee) a pickled vegetable dish from Korea

maize (MAYZ) corn

masa (MAH-suh) dough made from corn flour, used to make tortillas

Mesoamerica (mez-oh-uh-MER-i-kuh) a historical region from central Mexico to Honduras and Nicaragua

migas (MEE-guhs) a breakfast dish made of eggs, fried tortilla strips, and other ingredients

Nahuatl (NAH-wah-tuhl) the language spoken by a group of peoples native to southern Mexico and Central America, including the Aztecs

nixtamalization (niks-tuh-MAL-ee-uh-zay-shuhn) a method of treating corn to enrich the nutritional content

pellagra (puh-LAH-gruh) a disease caused by a niacin deficiency

prolific (pruh-LIH-fik) producing a lot of something

spit (SPIT) a rotating metal rod used for roasting meat

staple (STAY-puhl) a core element of a diet

taquitos (tuh-KEE-tohs) a rolled, deep-fried taco

tortilla (tor-TEE-yuh) a thin flatbread usually made from corn or wheat flour

INDEX

[21ST CENTURY SKILLS LIBRARY]